Thought Optional

Pointers Toward Consciousness

David Carlton

Sizzling Pan
Publications

For Raj and Mrs. Murphy

Commit

Commit to peace, to silence, to meditation. You have to want peace more than anything. Desire it, seek it, and then just be it.

Enlightenment

Reality in not an achievement or something to be conquered. It's always here. You don't have to rush to find it. You have your whole life for it.

Everything

You have to do everything as yourself. Everything.

Thoughts

Accept that the order and format in which your thoughts appear in your mind is utterly beyond your control.

Crack

Imagine if everyone around you was doing crack, and every time they offered it to you, you had to say no. That would be hard. From TV commercials telling you you're incomplete without a product, to social pressures reminding you that you don't look or act good enough, there is an infinite supply of "drugs" out there to create your conceptual self, and get you hooked on the idea of who you should be. At some point, you have to say, "No. I'm not interested. I don't do drugs." If you want peace, you have to take a stand.

Illusion

When you feel suffering, it's because you have created an illusion about what is. Most people do the wrong thing when they suffer. They cling to the illusion, and then leverage it by doing another thing that creates more suffering. If you keep levering up on the illusion, your next round of suffering will be more brutal and you will have farther to fall. The correct response when you are suffering is to be honest and look right at the illusion and your resistance to it. Being honest may create a moment of pain, but it also disrupts the flow of suffering and helps you see through the illusion. Don't cling to illusions. Ask what attitude or belief you have that is creating resistance to the illusion. The more effort and energy you put into an illusion, the deeper into it you will go, and the more pain and suffering there will be.

Redeeming

You really should never be angry. It might arise, but you don't have to attach to it. Anger really has to do with not taking action for yourself. If you are uncomfortable and you really care about something or someone, you will get out of the situation. Why stay in it and be angry. It's not redeeming.

Ownership

We are socially conditioned to automatically think about ownership. We see a commercial for a big boat with great styling and a powerful engine, and the ego kicks in and says "I should own it." That impulse isn't natural, and following it won't bring you lasting joy.

Tornado

We often think we're failing if we don't respond to our mind's demands. Our minds remind us, too, telling us we're weak or we'll never get it right. You don't have to identify with your mind any more than you would identify with the weather. It would be like saying tornadoes are stormy and wild, so I'm a loser.

Suspicious

People want to live in the valleys and not scale the peaks. They want to dwell where things appear reliable, secure and safe. They hope for, at most, a few big battles in their lives, preferably at times that are convenient for them. But that's not living in sync with reality. You should constantly challenge yourself and do scary things. Be suspicious of anything that works the first time. Take self-directed risks. Experience everything you do as a first trial run, and expect to move on. The universe will reward you for living your life.

Separate

Allow things to happen in the moment and pay attention to them. If you're busy making up and telling your personal story, you're not letting life happen. Let go of your story and allow everything. Separating yourself from what's happening, as a subject and object, will never lead to fulfillment. Nothing is separate and fulfillment is available in every moment.

Paperwork

The more truthful you are with yourself, the more naturally at peace you will be. If you actively seek the truth in every experience, it will transform you and make your days more relaxed. When you have a thought attack, don't try to find a clever way to escape. Unresolved thoughts pile up like paperwork on a desk. Don't ever run away. Face sensitive situations and uncomfortable thoughts by looking for the truth in them. It's much less scary than you think.

Numb

People tend to use delusion to numb themselves, because they're afraid of their own propensity to fail. Delusion stops you from feeling and keeps you stuck. You have to be really realistic about all challenges, because that's where all of the opportunity is.

Truth

Rather than dealing with sensitive issues, we often avoid the truth, creating bigger problems. It's better to look for the truth in your everyday experience. Move straight toward it in every situation.

Exciting

Their stories are the only things that people can control, and they like that. They make them big, or different, or simple or complex. Some people have a way above-average story, and some people's stories seem just perfect. The stories can be exciting, shocking, surprising or entertaining, but the stories can't create fulfillment because they aren't real. The stories are just spontaneously arising energetic thoughts that will go away like all thoughts.

Late

One reason people are angry is that they feel it's too late. They play the victim. They tell themselves there is little they can do, and everything is insurmountable. They aren't helpless. They are spineless.

Loud

The idea of being a loud and energetic person is popular in our extroverted culture. It reaps rewards in school and the workplace. Similarly, the mind gets loud and energetic to get attention, especially the more it's ignored. Remember that the loud and energetic chatter of your mind has nothing to do with who you are.

Pursuit

Constantly be in pursuit of good risks. Take a lot of them. It's the most direct way to determine what went right and what went wrong about something that matters to you, and the most direct and personal path forward.

Match

People are insecure and scared and out of their minds, hoping and praying that what spontaneously happens will match the story they have already decided on. It's an uncomfortable way to live.

Hug

Hug the present. Shake hands with it. You feel it and it feels you.

Afraid

When people are afraid they often go to their friends, and they all act afraid together. You should face fear yourself. Dive in. It has to be you on the line for the learning and growth to be memorable and meaningful.

History

Just because there's no statue or monument doesn't mean that history didn't happen for all of us, together. No one can claim it. It's not separate and we aren't separate.

Great

With everything you do, you want to be able to say "That went well, and I feel great about myself" or "That didn't go well, and I feel great about myself." Don't let outer circumstances alter your understanding of who you are.

Invested

People think they are in control of their world, and they aren't. They act as if they own whatever comes out of their mind — problems and emotions and ideas. They invest in them, with pride and insecurity, or by being a nervous wreck or making a fool of themselves. Once you claim ownership, you're invested. But why would you invest in something you don't own? Would you pay to put a new kitchen in your neighbor's house? See where you're feeling badly, and you'll likely see where you're invested in something you don't own. Then detach from the aspects of life where you don't have real qualities of ownership.

Big

It's best to pick a few big things that are important to you and dwell on them, and then get good at ignoring many other things.

Gasoline

Are you pouring gasoline on your personal story?

strategy

Drop all strategy. You don't need to constantly persuade yourself that the present moment is the most desirable place to be. You can exist in the moment just because you like the moment. It's yours. Let go and be in it.

Victim

Most people allow themselves to stay angry. They get comfortable being the victim, saying "The IRS is after me" or "These people don't like me". They separate themselves from the "problem" and keep the anger alive. They're really angry at themselves. They can't get to the fact that it's all one, that it's all arising in them and that it can all be solved through acceptance.

Volume

Dealing with pain is like knowing what volume of music you can tolerate as you sit in a bar. If you want to stay in the bar and try all of the drinks, what volume of music are you willing to put up with to reach your goal?

Cousin

Identify the parts of yourself that you're stuck with, for better or worse, that will never change. Note all of the ways you perceive things. Then shift the focus of your life to who you actually are. Follow your own standards, not your cousin's or your neighbor's. Know who you will be whether you lose a lot of money, or a leg, or win the lottery. Claim yourself. Make all choices based on who you are. If you don't, it's like being stuck with a parcel of land that you can't develop. Don't miss your own potential.

Thinking

Remember that existence is here, with or without your thinking.

Endless Supply

Do what has meaning to you. Try to get an endless supply of it. You never know how close you are to success.

sad

Being yourself eliminates fear, anger and anxiety. It can be sad sometimes, but it makes you free.

Reason

Thinking or speaking for no good reason is undesirable. Be present, without words or a strategy, and the right things will come to you.

Bricklayer

Don't engage your mind unless there's the atmosphere for it. What's the point of a bricklayer analyzing an opera, or an auto mechanic worrying about the meaning of a painting? Why would a mathematician stress about understanding Shakespeare? Dogs don't put effort into climbing trees because they're dogs, and elephants don't try to fly. Don't engage your mind unless there's a reason. Live as effortlessly as possible, and only as yourself.

Shock Absorber

Present moment awareness is a shock absorber. If you don't have a lot of mind activity, you don't need a big shock absorber. If you have constant mind activity, presence is a massive shock absorber. More mind activity, more presence.

Teacher

Angry, petty, bitter people who are addicted to thought can be excellent dark spiritual teachers.

Redemption

There's always a second chance if you accept that life is perpetual change. If you don't believe in redemption, you come up with excuses. You think that if you fail, you're done. You blame others and say you're at the end of your road, or the ship has sailed without you. How limited to think that you know your destiny is done. Always think about what's next, especially when you fail. Assume there will be failures and use them to absorb direct feedback. Become closer with the truth that's revealed to you when you miss your mark. Use yourself as a perpetual test subject in consciousness. Get very comfortable with your own failure process, and understand that it contains all of the mechanics of growth. Risk something every day and use the redemption cycle to move forward. That's what engages you with the world as a human being.

Radio

Think of your body as the vehicle by which you live your life, and your mind like the radio in it. The radio can be on at different volumes, and sometimes it's really loud, but remember that it's not your whole existence. It's just part of the vehicle in which your existence is installed. Focus on your existence, not your noisy mind. You can turn the radio off in your truck, and it will still be a truck.

Liked

Don't worry about being liked. Worry about doing what you want to do. That means you need to accept who you are and know what you want, and then go for it.

strawberry

The only truth is in your direct present experience, now. People mistake thinking for the experience. Take eating a strawberry. You can think about its size and texture, and the well designed supply chain that brought it to the supermarket. But for you, that's not what's real. That's the story. For you, eating the strawberry is the truth.

Revolving Door

If your pain is lasting, it's because you've made a place for it to stay. You're attaching to it. Just keep your revolving door open and pain will come and go on its own. Don't lock it down.

Awareness

All you have in the present moment is awareness of your awareness, and that's all you need.

National Park

At national parks, they don't make a lot of changes or let you litter. The parks are precious preserves. Weather events will happen and trees may fall down, but the park will still be there. Think of yourself as a national park, and don't touch your true personality. Don't alter it. Don't pollute it. Don't let anything toxic be dumped on you, or build extra things that blight your landscape. Let your personality relax and be what it is. Let people visit and enjoy it. Even in difficult times, let it be.

Marketer

Your mind is always trying to get your attention. It wants you as its full-time client. If the real you refuses, the mind loses its power over you. Don't succumb to the marketing of your mind. Watch it with amusement, but don't buy. You don't need to be represented by an agency.

Work

When you find the right type of work, you will love it when it's fun and stay in peace when it's not. You won't feel a need to complain when the work is really hard, and you won't find it intolerable when challenges arise. Look at the work you do as an opportunity to love yourself.

Nerve

People who have the nerve to be fully themselves are personally and professionally very successful. Everyone may not like them all of the time, but they get done what they need to get done, for themselves and others.

Present

Be fulfilled in the present. Then challenge yourself. Work hard. Feel the full intensity of the present moment.

Powerful

All pain can be turned into something powerful.

Allow

If you want something bigger, step aside. Let it come to you. Surrender to the flow. Have the discipline and compassion to surrender, and allow everything.

Mistakes

You should trust your mistakes. They teach you. They set you free.

Reason

Pain is a terrible reason not to be yourself.

Miserable

When we're not grounded in consciousness and are living from the ego, we go from chaos to tragedy to chaos. Opposites play out in an endless cycle. Here's how it goes. Chaos first. Things are booming with your job, but you're spending all your energy scrambling for more and more external rewards, and deep down you fear losing them. Then tragedy strikes. You're fired. You sell everything you can't afford, cry a bit, and then blame the company for ruining you. It's a miserable, dramatic time. Then you get another job and enter the next phase of chaos. You're relieved to have survived the first tragedy, but soon feel pressure to do even better than the last time. And on and on. It's a miserable way to exist. Wouldn't you rather live in peace?

sit

We can get away with not being present, and we usually survive. Modern life doesn't require presence as it once did when our survival depended on it. But real life is accessed through presence. It's important to practice reconnecting with our own existence. The best way to do that is through meditation. Just sit.

Present

Once you are present, emotions don't matter, and attachments get detached.

Welcome Mat

As long as there's no welcome mat for your emotions to stay, there's nothing to be afraid of when you feel them. If the moment scares you or hurts you, or has loss in it, the emotions will flow through you if you let them. You won't end up feeling damaged because you haven't attached to them. Remember that there is nothing wrong with feeling emotions in the moment, and then letting them move along their way.

People

Be around honest, present, ambitious people.

Conviction

Life is about having convictions aligned with who you are, and pursuing them through pain and pleasure. What is the quality of your convictions? Would you stand by them no matter what? If you don't have convictions, you'll revert to a default mode imposed by someone or something else, only to be swamped over and over again.

Disturbance

Once you are grounded in peaceful awareness, if it's disturbed then stay close to the disturbance. Don't go seeking. Stay grounded in it and realize that a concept you are attached to is creating a problem. Don't run off. Ask yourself, what part of my ego will burn off if I stay close to the discomfort? What resistance can I release? Let more reality in. At first it will be a trickle, then a river, then an ocean. Be in the ocean of awareness. Let the moments flow in.

Once

The hardest thing is for people to surrender, once. You have to know what it is to detach from a concept. Once you do, you can detach from any concept, and all of them. Once you are detached, you are in the flow and energy of life.

Airport

Do your thoughts and emotions always have a place to land? Do you provide an airport where they can fly in anytime, with a nice long, wide runway? If your ego is running the show, your landing strip will be huge. Your thoughts won't miss, and you'll be pummeled. You don't have to give your thoughts a place to land. Remember that a smaller target is harder to hit. Use presence to close your airport. Think of yourself as a jungle island where tourists fly over but can't land. Cruise ships can sail by, but passengers can't disembark. Use stillness to take yourself out of the ego game and let your thoughts and emotions pass on by.

style

Try to fill your life with activities that feel natural and meaningful to you. Experience your natural style as intensely as possible, and let others do the same. Life is all about directly experiencing your own natural tendencies, and always identifying closely with them. It's like seeing a "For Sale" sign outside a fancy, ostentatious house that isn't your style. Pass it by. Remind yourself that you don't want to own it or even be in it for awhile, because it will get in the way of you expressing yourself. Always stick with your style and don't confuse it with anyone else's. You'll be more peaceful and powerful.

Job

Money and stuff don't matter. They are byproducts. Peace is the real payoff. If you lose your job, stay calm and be yourself. Don't react to external changes in a way that disrupts your peace. There will be excuses, threats and worries as your ego reacts, but stay in peace and find other work that's in line with who you are. Instead of thinking of it as going from job to job, think of it as going from yourself to yourself. Move from purposeful peace in one place to purposeful peace in another. Don't bother identifying with the money or stuff. Stay in peace and the money and stuff will follow.

Surrender

Surrender is a combination of letting go of concepts, and using that space to allow all of the energy of the moment and all awareness to flow into you.

steroids

Don't work too hard to motivate others. It's like giving them steroids. Substituting your motivation for theirs masks the reality of who people really are, and wastes your energy. If you're working too hard to motivate others, you're making them more comfortable about not being themselves. When you drag others along, you're artificially helping them blend in as if they belong when they don't. It's exhausting, and it's not real or sustainable. Let everyone be themselves.

Important

When fear comes, all you have to do is ask yourself, are you going to do what's important to you or not?

Claiming

The thought "I am" is claiming. It's just a thought we believe to justify all of the others.

Screwed

No matter how high you move up the status ladder, or who you're with or what you're doing, you can always find evidence you're being screwed by somebody. Don't be mesmerized by the power of other people and things over you. Don't play the victim. Life is about becoming more yourself every day, and not letting obstacles or discomfort stop you, or even slow you down.

Money

When people complain about money, they're usually talking about their fears. It's not socially acceptable to say you're afraid, but it is to say that your bank account is low or the economy is bad.

Repossessed

Be dedicated and committed to living as yourself. Have a strong conviction about who you are, and understand how awareness moves through you. Even when pain seems to be lasting, it's really momentary and doesn't mean you're a failure. Don't ever link temporary pain to losing yourself or your sense of direction. It's not like, "Oh no, my car got repossessed today so I lost my soul!" They aren't linked.

Mercedes

Happiness often comes from observation, not ownership. When you watch a Mercedes commercial, that may be the most satisfaction you will ever get from the car. If you buy one, unless you imitate the whole commercial in your life — from the hairpin turns on the scenic road to the great music to the sexy babe in the passenger seat — watching that commercial will likely be the best experience you will ever have with that car. The joy doesn't come from owning the car, and being liable for it and having it repaired. The joy comes from watching the story about it in the commercial. Observe and be joyful, and understand that ownership and control are illusory and don't necessarily create happiness.

Boxing Ring

Picture one hundred people in a boxing ring. They're beating each other up. They punch one another, take a quick break, then jump back into the ring and go at it again. This is the ego mode of living. It wastes energy and exhausts us. We are constantly tempted to jump back into the ring to continue the ego battle. The question is, will you let yourself be tempted back in? Is that how you want to spend your energy, and your life?

Out of Control

Most people would rather be angry and in control, than at peace and out of control. Having no control in life seems scary, so people create personal stories that they think will make them feel safer. They say "This is how I want my/my kid's/my spouse's story to go", and then cross their fingers and hope for the best, clinging to their stories. There is suffering and gossip and misery when events don't quite match up, and a sense of control when things align. But there's no lasting peace. If people were really in control of life, they would be calm and relaxed, living without judgment, and they'd never worry about their own or anyone else's personal story.

Intended

Be sure you are using your life exactly as it was intended. One way you'll know is that when you are fulfilling your life's purpose, you won't feel a lot of panic or regret or fear.

Treat

Don't accept any treat the ego can give.

Accentuate

Always accentuate who you are. Try to put yourself in environments where you're at peace, and all your eccentricities and weirdness give you an advantage. Express yourself every chance you get.

Dream

Life can seem like a series of random events, which scares people, so they craft personal stories to imply control. If you have a bad dream, you don't wake up and think that you are a bad person. You understand that the dream came from a place outside of your control. It's the same with life and your waking dream. You don't control where your thoughts come from, and you don't need to make up stories to pretend that you do.

Achievement

Everywhere we turn, we are encouraged to achieve for external rewards. If you know who you are, those rewards have no meaning. If you know who you are, being yourself is the achievement. Everything you do has a unique meaning. That's the achievement.

Return

You can't give up inner peace once you know it. Once you've experienced it, you'll know it's always there for you and you will always return to it. Once you understand what it feels like, you won't want to exert energy outside of that arena, and life will flow with more energy and ease.

Coat Hanger

Know your personality. Be yourself. Understand how you perceive the world. Be aware of what always seems exciting to you, how you work, who you like to talk to, and who you can help. Think of yourself as a coat hanger and find the right coat to hang on it.

De-program

See what's happening now, in this moment. Everything else is just an idea. It's worth experiencing life directly so that you are not continually exhausting yourself with unreal stuff. De-program yourself of the social conditioning that you are supposed to feel good about this and bad about that, or worry about the future and the past. Be in every moment, and experience life as it is.

Water

Don't claim ownership of ideas and concepts. When we're first born, we don't know anything about ownership. Someone has to teach us. Babies just see matter moving through space. They don't think about owning stuff or worry about litigation to stake a claim to their possessions. So much of our adult life is predicated on ownership. We own cars and houses, then we try to own our thoughts and identity. We defend them with lots of our energy, and wonder why we don't ever feel quite satisfied. Drop the conditioning that tells us we have to own everything. Think of the zen guy who took water out of the river each day, and always poured some back to remind himself that it didn't belong to him. He didn't act like a European explorer, plant his flag and say, this is my water.

Lost

Get in the habit of getting fully lost in things. Immerse yourself and be fully with what you are doing in any moment.

Feel

Feel how you feel in real time, and let your feelings happen in the huge space of consciousness. Bring them on. If you feel overwhelmed, don't block them. If an emotion is chasing you down, experience it. Don't try to outrun it.

Freedom

Even though a lot of people don't see it that way, the point of meaningful work is freedom. Pursue it by working hard on what's important to you.

Splinter

Spirit is like a splinter and will work its way out one way or another. It wants to express who you are. You're lucky if your spirit is feisty and restless, because it will push itself out into the world faster. Express yourself, and always be grateful that you don't have a lazy, heavy spirit.

Joyride

Don't waste your life on a conceptual self that takes you on a joyride to nowhere.

Road Trip

The only thing that determines the quality of your life is your appreciation of the present moment. Moments will teach you and reward you. Paying attention in the moment is like knowing how to drive if you want to have a pleasant road trip.

Product

Awareness threatens our consumer society. If we actually understood that we were adequate as we are, that we were everything we could ever be in each moment, then no fashion, no cosmetic, no product and no person could ever influence us or make us feel that we were less than whole without it.

Civility

Be whoever you are. Have some manners. Manners make life easier. Civility helps keep people in the moment.

Hard Work

Hard work reduces you to the basics. It's clarifying. Hard work helps you learn, "This is me" or "This isn't me". Don't resist hard work. Throw yourself fully into everything you do and listen to what it's telling you.

Forget

Remember you will never fully understand anyone else and they will never fully understand you. Respect the other person's right to forget about you. Forget about others, then forget about yourself.

Control

You can be calm and focused and not have control, or you can be enthralled and dramatic and not have control. The latter wastes more energy, but either way reality doesn't change. Life is always just what's happening.

Telling

The mind is always telling you that you have an inadequate conceptual self and you should do something to be more adequate. There is a dramatic call to action to arrive at a better conceptual self, and if you get there, it's never good enough. The mind goes on and on because that's how it works. It doesn't ever want the game to be over.

Running

People are running around in all directions, or sometimes in the same direction, so that they can perhaps become fulfilled if they create the right stories for themselves. They tweak and propagate their stories in an effort to get where they think they want to be. They hope that once they match their personal stories, they'll feel fulfilled. But fulfillment never happens, because there is no real fulfillment that can come from a story.

Effort

Don't imply yourself in the effort you make.

Confrontation

When faced with confrontation, it's OK to say nothing
and use no energy. Just be honest with yourself about
how you feel. Violent, aggressive and angry people who
cross your path help show you parts of your personality,
but you don't have to engage with them or spend any
energy on them.

simple

Make everything you do simple and playful and present.

Addiction

Most people can't give up their minds. They're addicted. It's like a drug. If you can't recognize yourself as awareness, and not as your mind, you have an addiction to your self-concept, and you will live in fear.

Narrative

There is no separate self, and no one's personal narrative will ever be anything other than disappointing. Your personal narrative has nothing to do with reality. It cannot lead to fulfillment. There is no "you" to be fulfilled. The dynamic doesn't work. You're not separate, and you're not a story. You are consciousness expressing itself.

Concepts

Don't attach to or identify with a conceptual self. Follow your natural tendencies. Taking a side about who you are creates a separation that isn't real, and takes you out of the flow of life. Let your mind and body be as they are. Don't spend energy on creating or taming ideas about who you are. Just be the awareness that you are.

Bank Robber

Fearlessly let the moment come as it unfolds. Let it all flow through you. You have nothing to defend or protect. You didn't create the world and you don't control it. Open the door wide to consciousness and say "Come on in." You can let a bank robber in as long as there's no money in the bank.

World

You don't have to save the world. You just need to express yourself and embrace a desire to have a challenging adventure. Arnold Schwarzenegger wasn't that much better at weight-lifting than others. He just loved the experience of doing it. Arnold wasn't trying to change the world or make everyone proud of him. The work of weightlifting was meaningful to him in and of itself. Warren Buffet is another example. He's usually laughing and lighthearted. He does his work for the love of doing it.

Patterns

Pay attention to repeating patterns. They teach you about who you are. Get aligned with them, and don't fight them. Michael Jackson loved dancing. For him, every song represented an urge to dance. Imagine if he got mad at every person who turned on the radio, saying "Why did you turn it on? I'm so angry. It makes me want to dance."

Point

There's no point in not being present, and a big point in being present.

story

You cannot find fulfillment in your personal story. Ego stories don't lead to fulfilllment. It's not like once you get this or that, you'll be happy. When you realize that the mechanism of the ego won't do what you think it will, you'll be less interested in paying attention to it.

Run

Why run away from awareness? It's who you are. Isn't that enough? Would you rather run to a concept that's not real? Ask yourself why you're running and what you're afraid of.

Relaxation

Move away from tension and toward relaxation as much as possible. Let go of blaming the past. Let go of the future. Let go of all external stuff. Totally relax and let yourself automatically work at your own pace. It seems paradoxical, but you'll accomplish much more.

Evolve

Everyone has a radar, a knowing. Just watch. And meditate. It will evolve.

Trust

When you get scared, there is a strong tendency to look to others to tell you who you are. You keep getting burned and you think it's because you are not following society's expectations well enough, so you redouble your efforts and look to others for even more definition. But you can't resist who you are, and no one else can create who you are. When you're in conflict or faced with a fretful situation, don't look to society to define you. Why would you think anyone else has you all figured out?

Imagine

You don't have to imagine yourself with a story to exist. You don't need a thought about yourself to exist. You exist before you think.

Intangible

It's in the intangible, not the tangible, that human power lies.

unconditional Love

Why would you not want to be around people who love you unconditionally?

Simplicity

People say, "I'm not getting enough from life". They complain that they need more vacation, more clothes, more down time or more beer. Actually, people are getting too much out of life. They are getting lots of stuff. And they're also getting things that aren't even real, like dramatic struggles in their imaginations, superficial rewards with no meaning, and big self-concepts and stories that help them avoid reality. Appreciate and pursue simplicity. It's so much more for less.

Joy

To fulfill your potential, focus on things you want to be doing at the core your being, for the joy and fun and experience of doing them. Don't do something just to brag about it, or for other external reasons. Make sure that your commitments, at the core of your awareness, have meaning for you and seem beautiful to you.

Values

A person may be offended when you act in accordance with your values. As long as you don't intend to harm them, don't regret your actions. Others will experience their fair share of pain sooner or later, regardless of whether you interact with them and regardless of whether you offend them. Live your values every day.

Moment

The moment is intangible for the mind. It can't grab onto it. When you're present, the mind has nothing to do.

Disdain

How can people have disdain for their own existence. You're alive and it's your experience. Accept it, with love.

Drastic

The ego will take drastic measures to make itself seem real. It's like an imaginary friend that keeps poking you.

Senses

Just because you haven't taken it in with your senses doesn't mean you don't know it. People think that their senses are everything, and that they've used up all of their understanding once they have taken something in with their senses. The reality is that we take in just a little with our senses. We can't get it done with just our senses. Our ability to access consciousness is never over and is beyond our senses. Be open to watching what forces are coming together and what they are creating, and trust the deeper understanding that comes from below your mind and beyond your senses.

Jealous

Why would you want to make yourself feel bad by comparing yourself to other people? You could be jealous of birds because you can't fly, or jealous of a tree because it's tall and thin. If you don't do it with them, why would you do it with your neighbor?

Peak

You will never reach your peak level of performance until you are doing what you want to do for the love of doing it.

Talking

Bragging about our spiritual superiority, as in "I can meditate better than you", is just the ego talking. Since real enlightenment is beyond words, and there's no truth in thought, what do we think we're telling everyone?

side

It's not necessary to take a side with every thought, whether it's yours or someone else's. You don't need to get involved, and you certainly don't need to dramatize. Use your energy for the right things.

Hunt

The spiritual search is like hunting for terrorists. We say, "I'm going to hunt down my mind. I saw it and I'm going to chase it. I'll conquer it once and for all. No more ego and judgment for me." First there's surveillance, then seeking. We think we have the mind cornered. We interrogate it. We're sure that hard core spiritual seeking is going to take care of this menace. We climb a mountain, meditate another hour or find a guru, all to extinguish the mind. But the mind is innocent. It's just energy. It has no truth. It couldn't pick the truth out of a photo lineup. It doesn't know what to do. It has no strategy or plan. It's just a temperamental piece of machinery housed in our bodies. Once we get down that spiritual path, really close to the mind, we realize it was a long chase for nothing. We understand that the mind is a wild thing and a tool, helpful occasionally, but not something to rely on for the truth of our existence. Stop the hunt. No seeking necessary.

Approach

You have to see where the opportunities are for you. Be honest about who you are and know that if you approach things as yourself, opportunities are everywhere. The whole joy of life comes from expressing yourself genuinely. And if it wasn't somewhat of a challenge, you wouldn't express yourself.

Progress

There can be a difference between working hard and making efficient progress. Effort and suffering don't necessarily mean progress.

Weeds

Spending time "in the weeds" on things that are not important to you is a form of running away. It's an active avoidance of the critical activity of choosing what is most important to you. And the further you go into that valley, the harder it is to turn around. If you want to influence outcomes aligned with what is important to you, be very aware of where you put your energy and attention.

Barrier

Pain is not a barrier when you know yourself and what has meaning to you. Let it come and go like the weather. You can feel crushed or elated, but don't let pain stop you from moving towards your commitments.

Aware

Being aware is as good as or better than knowing what to do.

Funeral

Give your ego a funeral. Tell yourself that your made-up self is dead and it's not coming back to rule your life. Say goodbye to that unreal part of you that creates anxiety and fear and judgment.

Dolphin

Keep isolating what is essential to your personality. Notice what comes very naturally to you. Don't copy anyone. You can't start swimming like a dolphin and become one. To harness who you are, find the thing that you most want to do, and can be done with the least effort and most naturally for you. That doesn't mean you won't work hard at it. It just means it won't feel like "work".

Hurdle

A big hurdle is to keep asking hard questions of yourself, especially when you are afraid. Develop the habit and take the time to get your own answers.

Moon

You will come to an understanding that there is no truth in thought. Thought is just a tool. The truth is here and now, beyond thought and without concepts. Thoughts from many minds allowed us to engineer a rocket to take some men to the moon. Note that the blueprints, the flight checklist and the spacesuit design weren't the truth. Standing on the moon was.

Adherence

What we call confidence comes from a deep, religious adherence to the truth, and a willingness to commit to taking risks in pursuit of goals that are meaningful to us.

Leader

There are many benefits to being a leader, but one downside is that you have to take responsibility for everything that happens on your watch. Practice being a leader in your own life, or community or company. Develop a pattern of taking responsibility, even when an event was totally unpredictable. Learn to say, "I'm sorry, I didn't foresee that" or "I made a bad decision, and I'll try to do better". Develop humility. Don't let the river between you and taking responsibility for your actions get too wide.

Float

You have to know where reality is. Some people just want to float above it. You need to land the plane and walk every once in awhile.

Work

You'll know you are doing the right thing when you are working so intensely that you willingly and easily sacrifice all of the things you don't need.

Concept

The concept of who you are is just as ridiculous as any concept. If you were asked each day to write 5 sentences about who you are, and looked back at them after ten years, or even a week, you'd see that your concepts weren't solid. The mind is great at generating random buzzwords and stories, but we shouldn't rely on them.

Moving

Always be moving towards your commitments. No lounging around. No matter the social or psychological pain or anxiety, keep moving. Don't judge whether the experience is worthwhile based on pain or its absence. If it's your commitment, move forward. You'll feel pain and anxiety at some point one way or another. Don't let it paralyze you. Keep moving. Pain can't stop you. It can only hurt you. Don't be afraid of pain. It will come and go on its own. You keep going.

In Common

Worry about your own issues. Don't worry about having things in common with others. We can't all love the same movies or be from the same city or wear the same color pants. Let that go. Be yourself.

Calmness

People mistakenly think that in risky situations, you can't be calm, and that to be calm, you should avoid risky situations. But calmness and risk-taking go hand in hand in the human experience. They are naturally linked. You really won't feel calm in life unless you are taking risks to express yourself and unleash your potential. And you must remain calm in order to take those risks and truly evolve. Otherwise, you're living at some level of fear, drawn into society's collective undercurrent of dread, and scrambling to be the best of the most fearful. Stay in peace and take risks, rather than joining the worrying mob.

Truth

Tell the truth.   Let others find the meaning in it.

Failure

Stop looking at failure as a bad thing. It's necessary to
grow. It puts answers right there in front of you.

Hammer

The mind is just a tool. It doesn't know the truth any more than a hammer or screwdriver knows the truth.

Life

Life is not about one activity. It's about expressing yourself anywhere and everywhere.

Bus

When you're standing on a busy sidewalk and a bus passes, you feel good when it moves on. You prefer the silence. Listen for the quiet, and become so comfortable with it that you want to find it everywhere. If the opportunity to think arises, don't take it. Go back to the silence. Retrain your consciousness to gravitate to silence without thoughts. Change your gravitational pull to awareness. Always look forward to the next moment of silence and peace, rather than the next moment of thought. Feel comfortable leaving your thoughts behind.

Anger

Anger is just a non-relaxed form of sadness. It's better to cry for five minutes than be angry for a week, or a lifetime.

Default

Make being meditative, not neurotic, your default mode. Enlightenment is when you can't tell the difference between when you are sitting in meditation and when you are living your daily life. Life is a meditation. It starts in a quiet place, any time of the day or night.

List

Personal peace and self-expression should be on the top of your list for choosing a job. People don't usually see work as an opportunity for self-expression, or make it a priority. Their main priority for a job is usually money and perks, and they say that as soon as they get those, they'll be peaceful and free to express themselves. But it actually works the other way around. Freedom and peace come from hard work itself, as long as the work is a form of self-expression for you. To be meaningful and sustainable, your work needs to be aligned with who you are. If it is, everything you need will come to you.

Others

People are not really afraid of what others do to them.
They are really afraid of themselves.

Bomb

Think of dealing with reality like defusing a bomb that was dropped in heaven but didn't explode. Stay close to reality and defuse it in your waking experience, through meditation and by looking at what you are resisting. Look for illusion and try to see what's holding it together. Don't wander into speculation and opinion and judgment. The question isn't how to get away from the bomb, it's to see where you are resisting reality and harboring illusions. Once you understand, the bomb is defused.

Black Holes

Do what comes naturally to you, even if the outcome
seems totally unnecessary or irrelevant. Stephen
Hawking, Elon Musk, Mark Zucherberg and Bobby
Fisher all did what came naturally. Each of their
pursuits was glaringly unnecessary, and all ended up
being extremely valuable in ways no one could have
predicted. Stephen Hawking studied worms and black
holes in space that had no connection to people's
everyday lives. He pursued intellectual inquiry as self-
expression. There was nothing "global" or "heroic"
about it, yet he expanded our thinking about the
universe and ourselves. There was no lofty goal when
Mark Zucherberg decided to make a computerized re-
creation of the minutiae of real social interactions, yet
look at Facebook now. Work hard on what you
naturally want to work on, without judging it under the

"necessary", "practical" or "save the world" standard. Whatever you do will find its meaning in the world in ways you are incapable of predicting or controlling. And that's not your job. Your job is to do the work.

Parts

When you identify the real parts of you, stop putting energy into changing them. Otherwise, you're putting effort into self-consciousness and trying to compensate for who you are. That won't work. Have high standards, but don't put energy into things you can't change, even if it makes others unhappy or is inconvenient for them.

Ambition

Having a lack of ambition has become socially acceptable in our society. People promote happy hour and the countdown to the weekend more than work itself. If you love to work or have a lot of ambition, you're a buzzkill.

Privacy

Everyone's different. Some people thrive on the social scene. They're energized by a party, and doing things alone depresses them. Others prefer privacy. For them, a party feels like an intense challenge and doing something alone feels like a magic carpet ride. Figure out who you are and go where you want to be.

Appreciate

Don't focus on what you can't do, unless it helps you accept what you can do. Then make the most of who you are.

Turtle

Be like a turtle in a shell. Sit and watch. Be totally present. Have no desire to engage your mind if you're not in an environment where it is needed.

Miles Per Gallon

We all know that cars get different mileage depending on their speed, the stops and starts, the type of gas they're using and the driver's style. People's minds are the same. The degree to which we exhaust ourselves mentally can be different, depending on how we use our minds. If we try to use our minds for something other than the practical uses for which they're made, or listen to them chattering all day long, we won't go as far. Remember, if there's no reason to keep your brain running at full speed, don't. Its a useful tool for certain things when you need it, but it can't do everything. Monitor your mileage.

Confidence

Presence is confidence. You cannot be fearful in the present moment.

Excited

Most people get anxious and excited and emotional about events that have nothing to do with who they are. If they were grounded in who they are, they'd barely get excited about anything.

Renovation

Having big ego issues is like having a house that's inefficient inside and an eyesore in the neighborhood. If you want to live a better life, you should sell that house and buy the right one. Instead, many people just do an ego renovation. They rehab their ego bit by bit, seeking meaning outside themselves and creating stories. They'll say, "I'm enlightened now. I'm renovated. I'm more efficient. I gave my ego a good time, and got my ego some new stuff, and I can go farther and work harder." But they'll also still say, "I need to seek more answers. I need to invest more in my story. And why do I keep losing insight, or missing the point about important things?" Don't take the messed up version of you and fix it up a little. Let go of the old house and focus all attention on the awareness in you. That's the new house that never needs to be improved.

Resistance

People think if they resist negative thoughts and emotions, they will be safe from pain and worry. What they don't realize is that stress and neurosis actually come from their resistance and non-acceptance, the shutting out of the present moment, and not from the emotions themselves. Don't ever resist negative thoughts and emotions. Don't claim them either. Just let them be.

Peace

Deep peace is felt. It's when all the music stops. It's when the circus ends. It's when the hurricane passes. It's big and empty and beautiful beyond words.

Cheerful

Not everyone is meant to be cheerful. Some people have innate desires for other things, like truth, or quiet, or seriousness.

Signals

Life sends us many signals, and pain is one of the most common. Essentially, it's the universe pushing us to choose what's important to us. When faced with the pain of doing something or not doing it, be brutally honest with yourself about which is greater. If you are working hard at something that's really important to you, the pain of not doing it will be greater. Accept that there will be some discomfort either way. Be willing to tolerate it and don't blame anyone else. Be honest about which direction life is pushing you.

Important

Do what's important to you, no matter how you feel. There's nothing wrong with anxiety or fear. It's only a problem if it stops you from doing what's important to you.

Silence

Put yourself in a quiet place, like a library or nature or a car. You just need to find a place where no one around you is being neurotic. Sit in the quiet environment. Refrain from thinking, and you will naturally become connected with the present. Get comfortable with the silence. No strategy, no technique, no label. Just sit. When you stand up, take the silence with you wherever you go.

UPS

Think UPS. Don't let any bad mind "packages" be shipped to your spiritual "house". Don't accept delivery.

Setbacks

Setbacks are for learning and testing you. They ask of you, "Are you ready to be you?" "Are you ready to let go of your ego?" "Are you relaxed being yourself in this moment?"

Impulsive

Awareness inhabits your body, which has a mind. Minds do very impulsive things as they constantly try to attach to things. Your mind may be noisy and active, but remember it's not your existence. Just because your mind is carried away doesn't mean your existence is.

Imposing

This existence is here for you right now, even if you don't know everything about it. It's full of mystery, and there's a lot of truth in acknowledging our ignorance. It's much more honest to say you don't understand everything than to pretend. Release all thoughts and concepts in this moment, and let go of your mind's struggle to concoct stories about things beyond your understanding.

Couch

People want to respond to pain with anger or by running away. You can't. Even if you hide on the couch with a beer and donuts, pain will find you. You'll get heart disease. Feel pain, but don't be insecure about it. You don't have to beat people up or protest or do drugs or hide. Just accept pain and realize it's nothing to get upset about. It's just another thing you feel.

Bully

Your mind can only bully itself. It can bully your ego but it can't bully your existence. Over time, you'll realize that there's no point in letting an imaginary self push you around.

Practical

Presence is very practical. When you have more presence, you can do more. Happiness and other emotions use up awareness. Ideas and concepts take up space.

stability

Stability comes from allowing turbulence to flow through your body and mind.

Transition

Transition to a mode of witnessing. Say no to ego gratification. Prefer presence and stillness as you move through everything in life.

Fool

Your ego is a silly fool. Break off all commitments to your ego. It will be there, but you don't have to take it seriously.

stare

Face fear as yourself. Feel it fully. People avoid fear, or they panic about it or ignore it. Some people pump themselves up preemptively against fear, or go into attack mode. None of those responses work. It's best to stare fear in the eye. Know who you are and face it as yourself.

Witness

Be the witness, not the criminal.

Block

If you block thoughts and emotions with your ego, you can't relax or be creative or loving. Instead, you'll live in contracted desperation. And then you're at risk, because whoever offers you a teaspoon of sugar becomes your savior. That's not where you want to be.

Fish

If you think of yourself as a fish swimming in consciousness, you'll see that there's ego bait everywhere. Look at the worms but don't bite the hooks. Swim right by.

Feel

Don't think about what you're saying. Feel what you're saying.

Today

Each day, remind yourself that your goal is peace through stillness and presence. Don't focus on opposites like happiness, which is inevitably followed by sadness. Focus on things that have no opposite, beyond everyday emotions.

Contraction

Be sensitive to your emotions and let them hit you as hard as they can. Let your thoughts be as big as they want to be. Stay open. Don't contract or run. The enemy of awareness is not negative thoughts and emotions. They're harmless. The enemy of awareness is contraction. Contraction is an incubator for the ego, and more negative thoughts and emotions. Contraction makes the bad stuff boil inside and doesn't allow anything new to enter.

shift

Shift from investing in your own self-concept — my this and my that — to being present and observing your life.

  Don't invest in your story. With ownership you expect a return, and that's addiction to the self-concept. You'll be perpetually serving your story to deliver the proper return. As you observe without investing, presence will increase and your life will be grounded in peace.

Limitations

Don't fight your "limitations". Understand them. Build on them. Start where you are.

Bulletproof

Nothing can touch you if you stay open to emotions. If you don't contract, you'll be psychologically bulletproof. No up or down will make or break you as long as you let emotions come and go, and realize they aren't you.

Explosion

Think of a stick of dynamite exploding in your bathroom. Now think of a star exploding in the galaxy. Which is more destructive to the space it's in? The star is a bigger, more violent explosion, but there is plenty of space around it. That's what you want for your thoughts and emotions. Let them occur in an exponentially greater open, limitless space. You want your thoughts and emotions to explode in your galaxy. Don't box them in.

Velcro

Your mind is like Velcro, or a sticker bush in the woods.
It always wants to attach itself to something.

Energy

Get to where the energy is for you. What environments and activities energize you? What mode or way of being makes you feel most alive? When you find it, let everything else go.

Gas Pedal

The difference between success and failure is keeping your foot on the gas pedal. How well do you react to the pain/pleasure cycle on the road to accomplishing things that have meaning to you?

Conduit

If you allow things to be as they are, and observe rather than try to control, you become a conduit for everything going on around you.

Return

Once you are in your zone, doing what matters to you, you can stop taking it so seriously and let go. You're invested and if you keep going, you will get a return.

Lamborghini

If the creator of the universe has a car collection, we are God's Lamborghini. We're a fancy, high end vehicle in the divine collection. Fancy, but still just a vehicle.

Reality

Every person has his or her own sense of reality. Live
yours.

Editor's Note

The author has been talking to me about life, spirituality and the truth since he was three years old, and I have been taking notes. As time passed, themes emerged, no doubt molded by many challenges he encountered and his relentless commitment to being himself. The importance of presence, the mechanics of the mind, the value of quiet, the meaning of work, and the reach of human potential all recurred as elements in an ongoing outpouring of insights. Over the years, I have often shared his words without attribution, acting as a conduit for someone too young to have credibility with, or access to, those who heard them. I also found myself frequently referring to his words, scribbled on scraps of paper, before meditation or in times of turbulence, appreciating how they clearly and succinctly directed me into the present, pointing me toward the consciousness that is beyond words and reminding me of the deep peace and love inherent in our existence. Craving a summary version of this wisdom, I compiled this volume.

Laura J. Ketchum, Editor

About the Author

David Carlton is a senior in college. He enjoys thinking and talking about the connections between our behavior and consciousness, spirituality, presence, pain and peace.

Notes

CPSIA information can be obtained
at www.ICGtesting.com
Printed in the USA
LVHW111516061222
734684LV00017B/290

9 780692 986110